SCIENCE BASICS

WHAT IS LIGHT?

by Mark Weakland

a Capstone company—publishers for children
www.raintree.co.uk

Raintree is an imprint of Capstone Global Library Limited, a company incorporated in England and Wales having its registered office at 264 Banbury Road, Oxford, OX2 7DY – Registered company number: 6695582

www.raintree.co.uk
myorders@raintree.co.uk

Text © Capstone Global Library Limited 2019
The moral rights of the proprietor have been asserted.

All rights reserved. No part of this publication may be reproduced in any form or by any means (including photocopying or storing it in any medium by electronic means and whether or not transiently or incidentally to some other use of this publication) without the written permission of the copyright owner, except in accordance with the provisions of the Copyright, Designs and Patents Act 1988 or under the terms of a licence issued by the Copyright Licensing Agency, Barnard's Inn, 86 Fetter Lane, London, EC4A 1EN (www.cla.co.uk). Applications for the copyright owner's written permission should be addressed to the publisher.

Edited by Jaclyn Jaycox and Mari Bolte
Designed by Kyle Grentz
Original illustrations © Capstone Global Library Limited 2019
Picture research by Eric Gohl
Production by Laura Manthe
Originated by Capstone Global Library Ltd
Printed and bound in India

ISBN 978 1 4747 7085 9 (hardback)
23 22 21 20 19
10 9 8 7 6 5 4 3 2 1

ISBN 978 1 4747 7089 7 (paperback)
24 23 22 21 20
10 9 8 7 6 5 4 3 2 1

British Library Cataloguing in Publication Data
A full catalogue record for this book is available from the British Library.

Acknowledgements
We would like to thank the following for permission to reproduce photographs: Capstone Studio: Karon Dubke, 20–21; Getty Images: Dorling Kindersley, 7; iStockphoto: Petrovich9, 19, TommL, 9; Shutterstock: Fouad A. Saad, 11, Nor Gal, 15, Piotr Krzeslak, cover, saicle, background (throughout), Stas Tolstnev, 5, udaix, 13 (top), VectorMine, 13 (bottom), Wang An Qi, 17.

Every effort has been made to contact copyright holders of material reproduced in this book. Any omissions will be rectified in subsequent printings if notice is given to the publisher.

All the internet addresses (URLs) given in this book were valid at the time of going to press. However, due to the dynamic nature of the internet, some addresses may have changed, or sites may have changed or ceased to exist since publication. While the author and publisher regret any inconvenience this may cause readers, no responsibility for any such changes can be accepted by either the author or the publisher.

CONTENTS

What is light? **4**

Waves and particles **6**

Electricity, magnets and light **8**

Light and radiation **10**

A rainbow of light **12**

Cleaning with light **14**

Electricity from sunlight **16**

Other uses for light **18**

Light experiment **20**

Glossary 22
Find out more 23
Comprehension questions 24
Index 24

What is LIGHT?

Light is all around us. It pours from the shining Sun and glowing light bulbs. We see it every time we turn on a torch or gaze at the Moon. Light helps plants to grow. Without light, nothing would be **visible**. There is even light we can't see. We cannot touch it or hold it. So what is light?

visible can be seen

FACT

Nothing moves faster than light in empty space. Its speed through space is 300,000 kilometres (186,282 miles) per second.

WAVES AND PARTICLES

Light can be both a wave and a *particle*. Light travels in packets called *photons*. Light waves can bounce off things, like a reflection in a mirror. The waves stream through space in every direction.
We cannot see most light waves.

particle tiny piece of something
photon small bit of light

ELECTRICITY, MAGNETS AND LIGHT

Light is made by moving **charges**. Think of a ring on an electric hob. Charges moving through the hob make it hot, giving it a glowing red light. These same moving charges also make electricity. They make magnets push and pull.

charge amount of electricity running through something

LIGHT AND RADIATION

Light is a form of **radiation**. These rays of energy spread out as they travel.

There are many types of light waves, each with its own use. Together they make the **electromagnetic spectrum**. Visible light is only a small part of this spectrum.

radiation rays of energy that travel out from a source
electromagnetic spectrum range of light that exists across the universe

A RAINBOW OF LIGHT

Light waves have different lengths and energies. With visible light, purple has the shortest wavelength. Red has the longest. When we see light, it often looks white. But white light is actually made of all the colours of the rainbow.

THE ELECTROMAGNETIC SPECTRUM

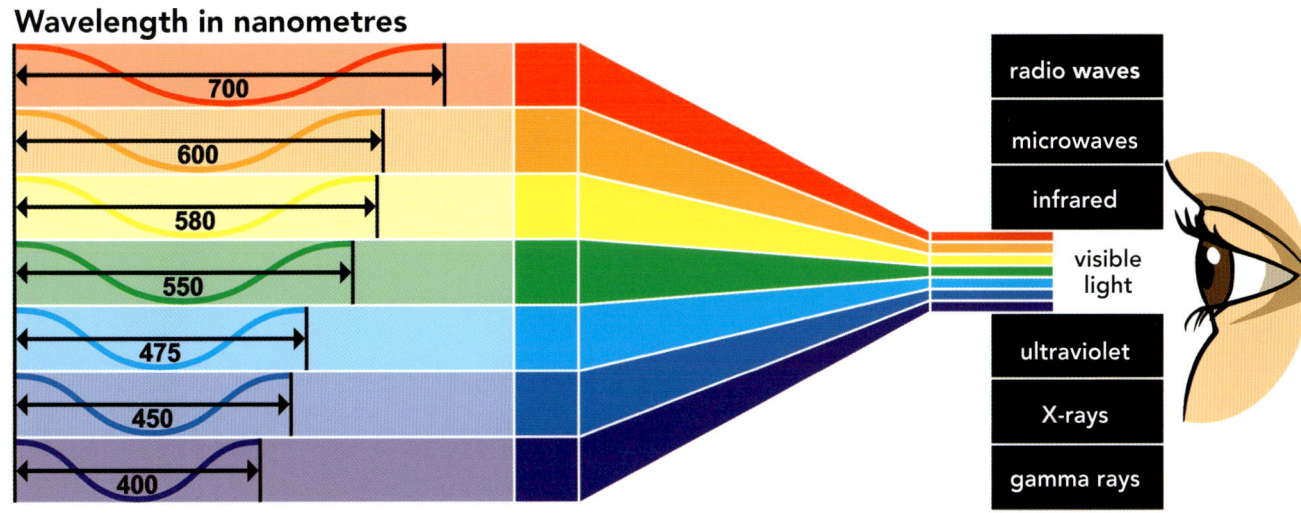

Wavelength in nanometres: 700, 600, 580, 550, 475, 450, 400

radio waves
microwaves
infrared
visible light
ultraviolet
X-rays
gamma rays

LIGHT AND WAVELENGTHS

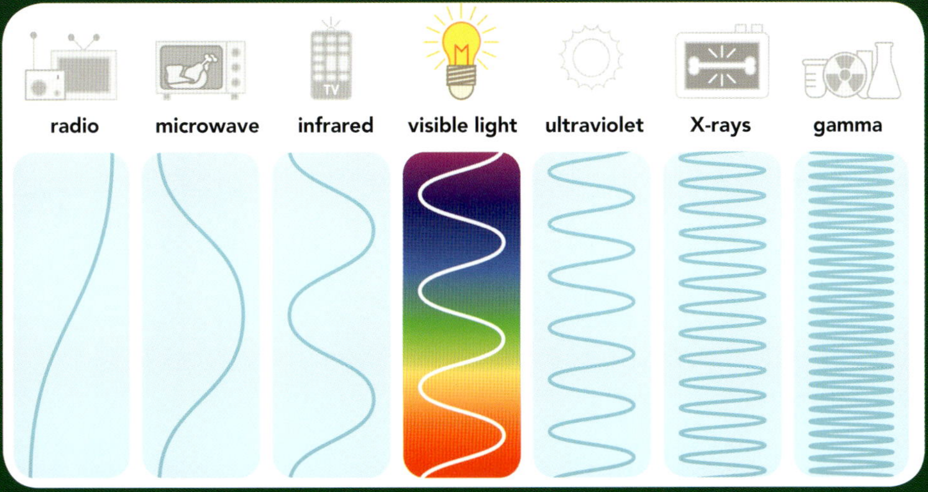

radio | microwave | infrared | visible light | ultraviolet | X-rays | gamma

Each type of light has a different wavelength. Radio waves are long. Some measure more than a kilometre. Microwaves are only centimetres in length. Visible light wavelengths are smaller than a strand of hair. And X-rays are even shorter.

CLEANING WITH LIGHT

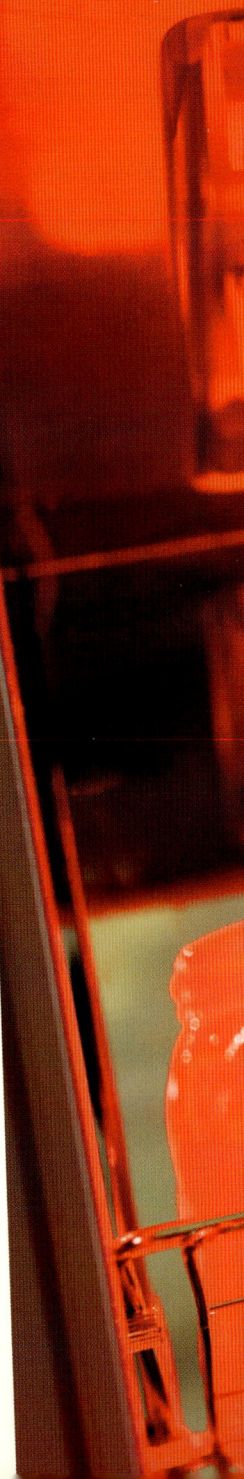

Ultraviolet (UV) light is good at killing germs. UV light comes from the Sun and from special light bulbs. Place a blanket outside in bright sunlight. The sunlight will kill the germs that live on it. UV light can also give us sunburn if we don't use sun cream.

ultraviolet light invisible form of light that can cause sunburn

ELECTRICITY FROM SUNLIGHT

Energy from the Sun's rays can be used to make electricity. **Solar** panels turn sunlight into electricity. Some people have solar panels on their homes. Solar energy is good for the environment. It does not produce any air pollution or harmful gases.

solar having to do with the Sun

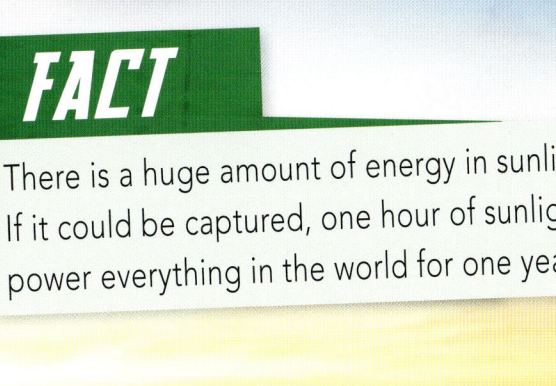

FACT

There is a huge amount of energy in sunlight. If it could be captured, one hour of sunlight could power everything in the world for one year.

OTHER USES FOR LIGHT

Laser light is very powerful. It is used in many ways. It cuts skin during surgery. It also stitches skin back together. DVD players use light from a laser. The light reads the disk. Then a computer turns the information into pictures and sound.

laser narrow, powerful ray of light

LIGHT EXPERIMENT

USE A WATER PRISM TO EXPLORE LIGHT

MATERIALS:
- a large bowl half filled with water
- a sunny window
- a small mirror
- a sheet of white paper folded in half or in quarters

WHAT TO DO:
1. Put the bowl on a table near the sunny window.
2. Put the mirror in the bowl, half in and half out of the water. Make sure the mirror is facing the light.
3. Hold the paper above and in front of the mirror. Move the paper until it catches the reflection from the mirror. Keep moving the paper until you see a rainbow.

WHAT HAPPENS:
The water and mirror make a **prism**. The prism breaks apart white light. It shows white light is made of many wavelengths. Each wavelength is seen as a different colour of the rainbow.

prism see-through plastic or glass object that separates white light into different colours

GLOSSARY

charge amount of electricity running through something

electromagnetic spectrum range of light that exists across the universe

laser narrow, powerful ray of light

particle tiny piece of something

photon small bit of light

prism see-through plastic or glass object that separates white light into different colours

radiation rays of energy that travel out from a source

solar having to do with the Sun

ultraviolet light invisible form of light that can cause sunburn

visible can be seen

FIND OUT MORE

BOOKS

All About Physics (Big Questions), Richard Hammond
(DK Children, 2015)

Light (Young Explorer: All About Science), Angela Royston
(Raintree, 2017)

Reflecting Light (Exploring Light), Louise and Richard Spilsbury
(Raintree, 2016)

WEBSITES

www.bbc.com/bitesize/articles/z2s4xfr
Learn more about light.

www.dkfindout.com/uk/science/light
Find out more about light.

COMPREHENSION QUESTIONS

1. How can we get light from electricity?
2. Light is all around us. In what ways do we use light? Write down as many examples as you can.
3. What do you think is the most important way to use light? Use evidence from the text to support your answer.

INDEX

charges 8

electricity 8, 16
electromagnetic spectrum 10

lasers 18

particles 6
photons 6

radiation 10

solar energy 16
speed of light 5
sunlight 4, 14, 16

ultraviolet light 14

visible light 4, 6, 10, 12

wavelengths 12, 13
waves 6, 10, 12